Table of Contents

Introduction

The key to successfully cannabis horticulture is to understand exactly how marijuana produces food and grows healthy. Whether grown indoors or outdoors, the requirements for cannabis horticulture remain the same. The basic necessities of cannabis are light, air, water, nutrients, a growing medium and heat to create the necessary energy to grow. Growing indoors, the requirements are the same, though it is necessary to be sure that you have the proper light spectrum, carbon dioxide (CO_2) and air circulation for cannabis to grow and thrive. When you have proper amounts of everything needed for proper cannabis horticulture the result is consistent and optimum levels of growth.Marijuana is normally grown as an annual plant, completing its life cycle within one (1) year so the seeds are planted in the spring and grown throughout the summer. Growing larger and larger until fall, the plants begin to produce flowers and create seeds to continue the full life-cycle of cannabis.In its natural state cannabis horticulture goes through distinct growth stages throughout its life-cycle.

One of the many beautiful things about the Cannabis plant is that it comes in many different variations.Not one marijuana type is exactly the same, and they also come in both the male and female variety. Some are tall and skinny, others are short and stout, and still, others are much smaller.The Cannabis plant is also known for its dioecious nature, meaning that it forms into distinct colonies of male and female plants. This is one of the reasons growers develop issues with male plants invading a grow room. In addition to male and female plants, growers and cultivators are likely to run into (and create!) hermaphroditic and androgynous plants. Whichever type of marijuana you ultimately choose to grow, it is a good idea to gain some basic knowledge of the variations and the differences between the different species, as well as male and female plants. You'll also want to understand the reasons why you'd want to separate them. When you know these things, you can make the best decision for your own growing habits.In this book, we will cover the three species of cannabis, the role of gender in growing as well as hybrid breeds and hermaphrodites.

There is actually no official scientific evidence that explains the differences between Indica and Sativa strains of marijuana or even confirms that these differences exist. Nonetheless, they are widely accepted facts among the marijuana growing and using crowd. There are some historical explanations for the beginnings of the Indica strain, also known as Cannabis Indica. It was first classified by Jean-Baptiste Lamarck, a French biologist, in the late 1700s. He also identified the fact that the plants were intoxicating. It was different from the regular hemp crops grown in Europe at the time, as they did not intoxicate the consumer. Because of the differences between the European hemp crops (then actually known as Cannabis Sativa), Lamarck named his Indian discovery Cannabis Indica to establish its uniqueness from the European hemp. It was considered a therapeutic remedy of sorts in Europe during the 1800s and commonly used in Western medicine.

Marijuana type 1: Cannabis Sativa

Sativa is the marijuana type that people seem to like smoking the most. This plant grows quite large, reaching up to 15 feet in some cases. While it is not a really thick plant, many growers like it due to how tall it can grow. Their leaves are long, dainty, narrow, and considering their height potential, these are perfect for outdoor growing. The seeds are soft to the touch, with no spots or markings on them. Do not expect this plant to flower quickly because Sativa takes its precious time, and even shifting the light cycles could have little effect on this. Sativa is usually found below a latitude of 30° N, in places like India, Thailand, Nigeria, Mexico, and Colombia. Sativa is often dried, cooked and consumed. While many people either vaporize or smoke this strain, it is the norm for users to use this to get high. It also can enhance your creativity, depending on the person. This is the strain you use when you want to be up and active during the day since it raises your energy and opens you up to fresh, new ideas. If you are an artist of some sort, you may love this one. Sativa is known for a high ratio of THC to CBN the two primary active ingredients in cannabis. Sativa dominant strains are higher in the THC cannabinoid. This makes it less likely to be used for medicinal purposes, but it is still common in Ayurvedic medicine. They also work well to combat the symptoms of:

• Depression

• ADHD

• Fatigue

• Mood disorders

Growing Cannabis Sativa

Cannabis Sativa is a type of marijuana that typically flowers for longer, has lower yields than Cannabis Indica, and has characteristically long thin leaves. They're taller plants in general since they come from a region near the equator, which has longer summers (which is also why their flowering period naturally lasts longer). A good thing about growing Cannabis Sativa is that the vegetative phase is shorter. There are even some Sativas out there bred to have shorter flowering phases. If you're from a hotter climate or have trouble keeping your grow room temperatures down, then a Sativa might be for you — they can take high temperatures better than Indicas.

Marijuana type 2: Cannabis Indica

Cannabis Indica is a more solid strain in comparison to Sativa, but it does not have the height Sativa achieves.

Indica strains generally grow between 3 to 6 feet tall (1 to 2 meters. It is a bushy plant with round healthy leaves, unlike Sativa. However, they both have marbled colored, soft seeds. Being that Indica is a short plant, this one is perfect for indoor growing. While Sativa takes some time to flower, Indica flowers much faster and can be influenced a lot easier by adjusting the light cycle to promote this phase. It is most commonly found above 30° N, in countries like Nepal, Lebanon, Morocco, and Afghanistan. The buds and flowers on Indica dominant strains will usually grow very close to each other and are stickier to the touch than Sativa plants. When you want to make hashish, Indica is the plant you would choose due to the amount of resin it contains. Cannabis Indica has lovely healing qualities, and helps with:

• Insomnia

• Alleviating pain

• Inducing relaxation of muscles

• Muscle spasms

• Calming anxiety

• Headache and migraine relief

• Growing Cannabis Indica

Cannabis Indica is a strain of marijuana that is typically higher yielding, has a shorter flowering time, and has leaves that are shorter and wider than a Sativa's. They're smaller plants in general, but they can get quite bushy. Lots of growers prefer growing Indicas for these reasons. Because of their shorter flowering phase, people who grow in colder climates with shorter winters may want to grow Indicas. Because of their shorter height, growing them indoors is also easy when it comes to growing Indicas.

Marijuana type 3: Cannabis Ruderalis

You will rarely hear anyone talking about Cannabis Ruderalis, which is one of the primary marijuana types and has a pretty short stature growing between 20-25 inches in height. Similar to Indica, this plant has very thick foliage. This plant is usually found growing in northern regions of the world. Ruderalis has an extremely early and fast flowering cycle because it grows farther north than any other type of marijuana and so doesn't have the luxury of a lot of time to mature before cold weather hits. Ruderalis is used to produce auto flowerers. One of the reasons you hear little about this strain is because it is not known to be highly psychotropic. It is used primarily as a source of additional genetic material by breeders and cultivators. That way, hybrids which flower early can be bred, and certain strains can be adjusted so that they will grow in more northerly climates.

Industrial Hemp Marijuana Types

Industrial hemp or hemp, typically found in the northern hemisphere, is a type of marijuana originating from the Cannabis Sativa species that is grown specifically for the industrial uses of its derived products. It is one of the fastest growing plants and was one of the first plants to be spun into usable fiber 10,000 years ago. It can be refined into a variety of commercial items including paper, textiles, clothing, biodegradable plastics, paint, insulation, biofuel, food, and animal feed. Hemp was a cash crop in America until the passage of the 1937 Marihuana Tax Act, partially because hemp can grow wild in climates where winter doesn't freeze the soil and kill the seeds. According to the USDA, hemp has a low THC content and isn't worth smoking. With THC levels below 0,3%, I totally agree.

Hybrid Marijuana Types

In modern cannabis cultivation and breeding, there are a huge number of varieties available. Many years of intense mixing and hybridization have created a huge spectrum across these three primary varieties. The different mixes all have different characteristics, running the gamut of possibilities relating to flowering cycles, yield, CBN:THC ratios, and disease resistance, among others. In general, the purpose of a hybrid plant is to combine positive characteristics from different strains together. Some key differences between Indica and Sativa marijuana types are the height of the plants, the length between buds, the size and shape of the leaves, the odor, the quality of the smoke, and the chemical properties themselves. In general, Indica is wide and robust while Sativa is long and thin.

Types Of Marijuana Seeds

There are few aspects of marijuana plants that are more important than the seeds. Everything begins with the seed, so you'd better make the seed count. In other words, you should carefully decide what type of seed you would like to buy. Let's look at some of the options.

Regular marijuana seeds

Regular seeds are, just as they sound, the normal type of marijuana seed that most people have traditionally grown with. These seeds will come with approximately 50% male and 50% female, so you will have to diligent about removing the males if you are growing with regular seeds.

Feminized marijuana seeds

These seeds are ones that will only produce female plants. These aren't naturally occurring — they need to be created to get them to be all female (which is also a marijuana grower's dream). Buying feminized seeds is the most efficient option for most marijuana growers.

Autoflower seeds

Seeds that autoflower are not photosensitive, instead they start to flower based on timing. In other words, they flower automatically. These can work really well for growing all year round, although it doesn't make much sense for indoor growers who already can decide when they want their plants to begin flowering by manipulating the light cycle. Once the plant is fully grown you will need to start thinking about harvest time. Our free little Harvest Guide will help you determine the best moment to cut your plants.

Male Cannabis Plants

When male-sexed cannabis plants finish maturing, the flowering process occurs all across the plant. Tiny racemes (short flower stalks) are formed at the base of the flower itself. When the flowers open, the plant releases a load of airborne pollen which sticks to and is absorbed by the pistil of the female plant. This is a basic explanation of how the fertilization and reproductive process in cannabis plants works. It can be difficult to distinguish between male and female plants at times, but the male usually has earlier sexual development.

Female Cannabis Plants

Like male cannabis plants, mature females will also produce racemes. In the case of the female plants, the racemes are a blend of tiny pistils and calyces (calyx). In each of the calyces, there is an ovule, which acts as the receptor for the pollen from the male plant. When the grains of pollen stick to a pistil, the pistil stalk then pushes into the calyx, and the plant is fertilized. The calyx itself is also the site where cannabis seeds are grown after fertilization. Each seed will have a mix of characteristics coming from both parent plants, as in other instances of sexual reproduction. The only time this wouldn't be the case would be if the parent plants were identical, as in the case of certain pure clones or specific hybridizations.

Hermaphrodite Cannabis Plants

Although rare as a natural occurrence in nature, many growers might be exposed to the existence of hermaphroditic plants, that is, plants that contain both male and female sex organs. These sorts of plants can fertilize themselves, which is both extremely interesting and potentially quite useful from a breeding perspective. In general, a hermaphrodite cannabis plant falls on one of the three points along a sexual spectrum. If the plant is mainly comprised of male flowers or has a roughly equal number of male/female flowers, it is probably of little use to a grower. If the hermaphrodite has mainly female flowers, however, it should definitely be saved. The pollen from these plants can be quite useful, and some growers collect the pollen because even though it is a male part of reproduction, the hermaphroditic pollen is genetically female, and will produce female flowers. In the '70s, Indica strains were brought to the USA and mixed with the already present Sativa plants, which set off a long chain of breeding and experimentation with cannabis cultivation and hybridization. It's important to note that despite the differences between all of these types of marijuana, they are essentially one species. They can still be bred together. The names Indica and Sativa refer to the areas where the plants are originally from. The same sort of idea is found in other agriculture, or dog breeds, where there is a wide difference in appearances, but the species are still the same.

The Sinsemilla Growing Technique

Sinsemilla is a type of growing marijuana where only female plants are allowed to blossom. This is done so that male plants don't get the opportunity to fertilize the females. This is done because many growers don't want seeds in their plants at all, although there are always exceptions. It's highly advised to keep grow rooms and male pollen as far apart as possible unless there is some express purpose for fertilizing the plants. The yield will drop substantially, and the taste of the plant will be ruined. In general, it's highly desirable to have unpollinated female plants, because more of the energy is devoted to producing cannabinoids and buds that are valuable to the grower, rather than being expended on sexual reproduction organs and seeds. Unpollinated plants will have more sugar, THC, and much denser more odorous flowers. This is ideal, especially for medicinal purposes, where the efficiency is very important for any patients who are in need of the active ingredient.

Growing Hybrids

Hybrids can vary greatly, but usually, they have some of the good qualities of both Sativas and Indicas. Because of the range of genes you can find in hybrid marijuana plants, it's hard to specify a common height, leaf shape, or other distinguishing detail. However, hybrids are often bred to have higher yields and be more pest-resistant, which is great for growers. Hybrids are extremely popular. Most of the seeds available are hybrids. To know what you can expect, be sure to read the growth descriptions before buying.

THC And CBD

You've likely heard of CBD and THC before. These two substances are the reason behind all the hype surrounding marijuana. There are some significant differences between the two of them, so let's look at what each of them does.

THC

The abbreviation "THC" stands for Tetrahydrocannabinol. It provides the psychoactive effects of marijuana, affecting the brain more than the body. Another substance, called anandamide, is mimicked by THC to make the brain function differently with memories, higher cognitive processes, and fine motorics. It also affects pain, fertility, hunger, and depression. Plenty of people choose strains of marijuana that are high in THC for its medicinal benefits.

CBD

Cannabidiol, or CBD, is another psychoactive substance that is commonly used in medical marijuana. The two interact, with the CBD having an influential effect on the THC, meaning they could strengthen or weaken certain effects of THC. Suppressing the psychedelic effects, for example, can be a big plus in a medicinal strain of marijuana. These are in no way the only two types of cannabinoids. The other ones, however, are only present in smaller amounts.

Marijuana Germination

In the germination stage, after about 3 – 7 days, the seedlings sprout white-colored roots and begin to establish their root system in this stage of cannabis horticulture. Soon thereafter they were to grow stems and develop their first few leaves. Moisture, heat, and air are the activators of the seed hormones (cytokinins, gibberellins, and auxins) during the germination life cycle of marijuana seeds. The hormones of the seed reside within the durable outer coating of the seed and the hormone cytokinin triggers cells to form and tells the gibberellins to grow in size. The embryo of the seed expands in size, utilizing the supply of food stored within the seed for growth.

Cannabis Seedling Growth

A single tap-root is produced from the germination of the seed as it grows down through the soil or growing medium and then the root systems begin to branch out. While the roots grow below the surface, the stem branches upward, above the ground in search of the light for its growth. Tiny rootlets in the root system draw in water and nutrients as the root system develops in size, helping to anchor the plant and create a foundation for its future growth. Seedlings need to receive about 16-18 hours of light for healthy, vigorous growth in the beginning stages of cannabis horticulture.

Marijuana Vegetative Growth

During this stage of cannabis horticulture, the plants need a minimum of 16 hours of light to stay in the vegetative state; though a maximum lighting time of 24 hours a day, 7 days a week can also be used. In cannabis horticulture, as the plant matures, their root systems take on specialized roles – the center, older and more mature roots contain a water transport system that may also store food for the plant. The tips of the roots extend and push deeper and farther into the soil in search of nutrients and water to supply its growth. These single-celled root hairs are the essential key for the plants to be able to uptake water and nutrients for growth. The roots are extremely delicate and must be handled as quickly, gently, and carefully as possible if doing any kind of transplanting since they are prone to dry up and die very easily if they lack water. They may also be damaged by open air and sunlight if exposed for too long. Similar to its root system, the cannabis' stem grows and stretches higher and farther to catch more sunlight. In cannabis horticulture the plants will produce nodes and buds along its stem – depending if it is Sativa- or Indica-dominant strain – the nodes will be at varying distances between each node.The central stem's primary function is to transfer water and nutrients from its delicate root hairs up and throughout the entire cannabis plant. Lateral and side branches continue to branch out to develop buds and for the leaves to capture light.

Cannabis Pre-Flowering

Pre-flowers will begin to show around the fourth week into vegetative growth, depending on the strain in cannabis horticulture. It is around this time that you will usually be able to determine the sex of the plant. Between the fourth and sixth node is where you will usually be able to find the pre-flowers of the cannabis plant. The male cannabis plant will develop tiny, smooth, egg-shaped pollen sacks while the female cannabis plant will develop small V-shaped white or pink hairs called pistils. Sometimes it may be hard to tell which are male and female. If you are unsure then you can grow them for a longer period of time to ensure you are able to correctly identify the plant's sex (male or female). If you want to ensure a seedless crop (sinsemilla), you will want to be sure to remove all males from your crop.

Marijuana Flowering

In natural growing environment outdoors, cannabis begins to flower in the fall when the days become shorter. Flowers begin to form during this last stage of growth, where leafy growth within the plant slows and flowers begin to form. The changing of the seasons signal hormone changes within the plant so they go from being in a vegetative state into a flowering or blooming stage of their life-cycle. Seasonal changes and the flowering cycle of cannabis horticulture are in direct correlation to the light spectrum of the sun and the amount of time (or hours) the sun is out each day. The flowering of cannabis is triggered by 12-hours of darkness and 12-hours of light every 24 hours. When left un-pollinated female flowers to develop without seeds, called 'sinsemilla'. Otherwise, when a female plant is fertilized with male pollen, the female flower buds will begin to develop seeds.

Mother Plants

Growers select strong, healthy, potent mother plants they know are female. Mothers are given 18-24 hours of light daily so they stay in the vegetative growth stage. Growers cut branch tips from the mother plants and root them. The rooted cuttings are called "clones." Cultivating several strong, healthy mother plants is the key to having a consistent supply of all-female clones. Any plant can be cloned, regardless of age or growth stage. Take clones from mother plants that are at least two months old. Plants cloned before they are two months old may develop unevenly and grow slowly. Clones taken from flowering plants root quickly but require a month or longer to revert back to vegetative growth. Such rejuvenated clones occasionally flower prematurely, and buds are more prone to pest and disease attacks. Any female can become a mother. She can be grown from seed or be a clone of a clone. I interviewed several growers who made clones of clones more than 20 times! That is, clones (C-1) were taken from the original female grown from seed. These clones were grown in the vegetative stage, and clones (C-2) were taken from the first clones (C-1). Blooming was induced in (C-1) two weeks later and (C-2), grown in the vegetative stage. Then, clones (C-3) were taken from the second clones (C-2). This same growing technique is still going on with clones of clones well past (C-20) and there has been no apparent breakdown in the potency or the vigor of the clone. However, if mothers suffer stress, they produce weak clones. Mothers that are forced to flower and revert back to vegetative growth not only yield less, they are stressed and confused. Clones that grow poorly are generally the result of poor, unsanitary cloning practices. A clone is an exact genetic replica of the mother plant. Each mother's cell carries a DNA blueprint of itself. Radiation, chemicals, and poor cultural practices can damage this DNA. Unless damaged, the DNA remains intact. A female plant will reproduce 100 percent females, all exactly like the mother. When grown in the exact same environment, clones from the same mother look alike. But the same clones subjected to distinct environments in different grow rooms will often look different. A six-month old plant produces more cannabinoids than a one-month old plant.

By cloning, a horticulturist is planting a THC-potent plant that will continue to grow in potency at a very rapid rate. A month-old rooted clone acts exactly like a four-month-old plant and can be induced easily to flower with a 12-hour photoperiod. Keep several mother plants in the vegetative stage for a consistent source of cloning stock. Start new mothers from seed every year. Give mother plants 18-24 hours of light per day to maintain fast growth. For best results, give mothers about ten percent less nitrogen, because less nitrogen promotes rooting in clones.

Cloning

Branch tips are cut and rooted to form clones. Clones take 10-20 days to grow a strong healthy root system. Clones are given 18-24 hours of light so they stay in the vegetative growth stage. Once the root system is established, clones are transplanted into larger containers. Now they are ready to grow for 1-4 weeks in the vegetative growth stage before being induced to flower. Marijuana can be reproduced (propagated) sexually or asexually. Seeds are the product of sexual propagation; cuttings or clones are the result of asexual or vegetative propagation. In its simplest form, taking a cutting or clone involves cutting a growing branch tip and rooting it. Technically, cloning is taking one cell of a plant and promoting its growth into a plant. Marijuana growers commonly refer to a clone as meaning a branch of a cannabis plant that has been cut off and rooted. Cloning reduces the time it takes for a crop to mature. Productive growers have two rooms, a vegetative/cloning room, about a quarter the size of a second room used for flowering. Smaller vegetative plants take up less space than older flowering plants. For example, a 250-or 400-watt metal halide could easily illuminate vegetative plants and clones that would fill a flowering room lit by three 600-watt HP sodiums. If the halide is turned off, fluorescent and compact fluorescent lamps are more economical and work well to root clones. Combine eight-week flowering/harvest cycles with continuous cloning to form a perpetual harvest. One easy-to-implement scenario is to take two clones every four days, and harvest one ripe female every other day. Every time a plant is harvested, one or two rooted clones are moved from a constantly supplied vegetative room into the flowering room. This regimen gives a grower 30 flowering clones that are on a 91-day schedule. It takes 91 days from the time a clone is cut from the mother plant until the day it is harvested. Using this schedule, a grower would have 30 clones, 10 vegetative plants, and 30 flowering plants growing at all times.

Cloning: Step-By-Step

Step One: Choose a mother plant that is at least two months old. Some varieties give great clones even when pumped up with hydroponics and fertilizer. If a variety is difficult to clone, leach the soil with two gallons of water for each gallon of soil every morning for a week before taking clones. Drainage must be good. Or mist leaves heavily with plain water every morning. Both practices help wash out nitrogen. Do not add fertilizer.

Step Two: With a sharp blade, make a 45-degree cut across firm, healthy 0.125-0.25-inch-wide (3-6 mm) branches, two to four inches (3-5 cm) in length. Take care not to smash the end of the stem when making the cut. Trim off two or three sets of leaves and growth nodes so the stem can fit into the soil. There should be at least two sets of leaves above the soil line and one or two sets of trimmed nodes below ground. When cutting, make the slice halfway between the sets of nodes. Immediately place the cut end in water. Store cut clones in water while making more clones.

Step Three: Rockwool and Oasis™ root cubes are convenient and easy to maintain and transplant. Fill small containers or nursery flats with coarse, washed sand, fine vermiculite, soilless mix, or, if nothing else is available, fine potting soil. Saturate the substrate with water. Use an unsharpened pencil, chop stick, nail, etc., to make a hole in the rooting medium–a little larger than the stem. The hole should stop about one-half inch (1.5 cm) from the bottom of the container to allow for root growth. Place a tray containing rooting cubes or plugs into a standard nursery rooting flat. If none exist, make holes through three-fourths of the cube for clone stems. Fill rockwool tray with water, pH 5-6. Always use strong plastic trays.

Step Four: Use a rooting hormone, and mix (if necessary) just before using. For liquids, use the dilution ratio for softwood cuttings. Swirl each cutting in the hormone solution for 5-15 seconds. Place the cuttings in the hole in the rooting medium. Pack rooting medium gently around the stem. Gel and powder root hormones require no mixing. Dip stems in gels as per instructions or roll the stem in the powder. When planting, take special care to keep a solid layer of hormone gel or powder around the stem when gently packing soil into place.

Step Five: Lightly water until the surface is evenly moist. Keep cuttings moist at all times. Clones have no roots to bring water to leaves. Water arrives from leaves and the cut stem until roots can supply it. Water as needed to keep growing medium evenly moist. Do not let it get soggy.

Step Six: Clones root fastest with 18-24 hours of fluorescent light. If clones must be placed under an HID, set them on the perimeter of the garden so they receive less intense light; or shade them with a cloth or screen. A fluorescent tube six inches (18 cm) above clones or 400-watt metal halide 4-6 feet (1.2-1.8) away supplies the perfect amount of light for clones to root. Cool white fluorescents (or a combination of warm and cool white) are excellent for rooting.

Step Seven: Clones root fastest when humidity levels are 95-100 percent the first two days and gradually reduced to 80-85 percent during the following week. A humidity tent will help keep humidity high. Construct the tent out of plastic bags, rigid plastic, or glass. Remember to leave openings for air to flow in and out so little clones can breathe. If practical, mist clones several times a day as an alternative to the humidity tent. Remove any sick, rotting, or dead foliage. Cut leaves in half to lower transpiration surface and to keep them from overlapping. Moisture that could foster fungus is often trapped between overlapping leaves. Keep the grow medium evenly moist so there is enough moisture to prevent cut leaves from bleeding out plant sugars that attract diseases.

Step Eight: Clones root faster when the growing medium is a few degrees warmer than the ambient air temperature. A warmer substrate increases underground chemical activity, and lower air temperature slows transpiration. For best results, keep the rooting medium at 75-80°F (24-27°C). Growing medium temperatures above 85°F (29°C) will cause damage. Keep the air temperature 5-10°F (3-5.5°C) cooler than the substrate. A warmer growing medium coupled with cooler ambient temperature slows diseases and conserves moisture. Misting clones with water also cools foliage and slows transpiration to help traumatized clones retain moisture unavailable from nonexistent roots. Put clones in a warm place to adjust air temperature and use a heat pad, heating cables, or an incandescent light bulb below rooting cutting.

Step Nine: Some cuttings may wilt but regain rigidity in a few days. Clones should look close to normal by the end of the week. Cuttings that are still wilted after seven days may root so slowly that they never catch up with others. Cull them out, or put them back into the cloning chamber to grow more roots.

Step Ten: In one to three weeks, cuttings should be rooted. Signals they have rooted include yellow leaf tips, roots growing out drain holes, and vertical growth of the clones. To check for root growth in flats or pots, carefully remove the root ball and clone to see if it has good root development. For best results, do not transplant clones until a dense root system is growing out the sides and bottom of rooting cubes. Cuttings are always strong and healthy-looking after you take them. After five or six days, leaves may start to change color. Leaves stay small and often turn a deeper shade of green. After about a week, lower leaves may start to yellow if their nutrient levels dissipate. A week after being taken, clones' stems will develop stubby callused roots called primordia. The primordia are semitransparent to white and should look healthy. Clones produce very little green growth during this process. Once the root and vascular transport system is in place and working properly, clones are able to experience explosive growth with the proper care. Rooting clones can handle increasingly more light as roots grow. Move the fluorescent lamps to two to four inches above plants when roots form. Fertilize with a mild fertilizer solution when all clones have started vegetative growth. Any sign of slime, pests, or disease means there are problems, and clones should be removed from the garden. Transplant only the strongest, well-rooted clones. Slow-rooting clones should be kept in the cloning chamber or culled out. Do not move clones below bright light until they have fully developed root systems. Once transplanted, clones are ready to harden-off. Set up a vegetative pre-growing area that is lit with an HID or bright compact fluorescent lamp for the rooted clones. Place them in this area to let them grow the first week or two of vegetation. This area needs to be just big enough to accommodate plants from the time they are a few inches tall until they are about a foot tall and ready to be moved into the flowering room.

When plants are too big for their containers, they must be transplanted to continue rapid growth. Inhibited, cramped root systems grow sickly, stunted plants. Signs of root bound plants include slow, sickly growth and branches that develop with more distance between limbs. Severely rootbound plants tend to grow straight up with few branches that stretch beyond the sides of the pot. To check for rootbound symptoms, remove a plant from its pot to see if roots are deeply matted on the bottom or surrounding the sides of the pot. When growing short plants that reach full maturity in 90 days, there is little need for containers larger than three gallons (11 L). Large mother plants will need a large pot if they are kept for more than a few months. Transplant into the same type or similar growing medium; otherwise, a water pressure differential could develop between the different mediums, which slows water movement and causes slow root growth. Starting seeds and clones in root cubes or peat pots makes them easy to transplant. Set the cube or peat pot in a hole in the growing medium, and make sure growing medium is in firm contact. Remember to keep root cubes and substrates evenly moist after transplanting. Transplanting is the second most traumatic experience after cloning. It requires special attention and manual dexterity. Tiny root hairs are very delicate and may easily be destroyed by light, air, or clumsy hands. Roots grow in darkness, in a rigid, secure environment. When roots are taken out of contact with the soil for long, they dry up and die. Transplanting should involve as little disturbance to the root system as possible. Water helps the soil pack around roots and keeps them from drying out. Roots need to be in constant contact with moist soil in order to supply water and food to the plant. After transplanting, photosynthesis and chlorophyll production are slowed, as are water and nutrient absorption via roots. Transplant late in the day so transplanted plants will have all night to recover. Transplants need subdued light, so foliage can grow at the rate roots are able to supply water and nutrients. Give new transplants filtered, less-intense light for a couple of days. If there is a fluorescent lamp handy, move transplants under it for a couple of days before moving them back under the HID or outdoors to harden-off. Ideally, plants should be as healthy as possible before being traumatized by transplanting. But, transplanting a sick, rootbound plant to a bigger container has cured more than one ailing plant. Once transplanted, cannabis requires low levels of nitrogen and potassium and increased quantities of phosphorus. Any product containing Trichoderma bacteria or Vitamin B1 will help ease transplant shock. Plants need a few days to settle in and re-establish a solid flow of fluids from the roots throughout the plant. When transplanted carefully and disturbed little, there will be no signs of transplant shock or wilt.

Pests And Predators

Frogs and Toads

Frogs and toads eat insects and slugs. The frogs will need a water source, while toads are more terrestrial. Large snakes in the garden will eat gophers, squirrels, and mice as well as the moles and shrews. Snakes can give you a good scare if you come across one unexpectedly! The snake will also want to eat your frog. Plan carefully before committing to any mini-predator solution to pest infestation.

Birds

Although most birds are welcome guests in most gardens, there are some that can make quick work of tender seedlings or new clones. The most effective way to keep birds from freshly planted seed and transplants is to cover plants with plastic wire or plastic netting. When installing the netting, make sure it is securely fastened around the perimeter of plants so hungry birds do not get underneath.

Moles

Moles are minor pests. They are primarily insectivores that eat cutworms and other soil grubs, but their tunnels may dislodge cannabis roots. Repel moles with castor plants or gopher (mole) plants (Euphorbia lathyris). Castor bean leaves and castor oil, as well as applications of tobacco and red pepper, will repel moles if put into their main runs. Blend two tablespoons (3 cl) of castor oil with three tablespoons of dish soap concentrate and ten tablespoons (18 cl) of water. Mix in a blender. Use this as a concentrate at the rate of two tablespoons per gallon (4 ml per liter) of water. Apply as a soil drench directly over mole holes. Barrel traps, scissor traps, and guillotine traps are effective and kill moles instantly.

Gophers

Pocket gophers are small burrowing rodents that eat plant roots and foliage. These herbivores find fleshy roots a real treat and occasionally attack cannabis. Should a family of gophers move into your area, get rid of them as soon as possible! Females can bear up to five litters of four to eight offspring a year. A family of gophers can clean out a large garden in a matter of weeks. The only sure way to get rid of gophers is by trapping. There are several gopher traps available, including ones that capture them alive. It will take some skill before you are regularly able to catch gophers with traps. You must avoid getting human scent on any part of the traps. If gophers sense the human odor, they will simply push soil over the trap to spring it or render it otherwise ineffective. Traps are put in gopher runways and so don't need to be baited. A fence of poultry wire or 0.5-inch (1.5 cm) hardware cloth buried one foot (30 cm) deep and standing 3 feet (90 cm) above the ground will exclude gophers. Line planting holes with chicken wire before filling with soil. Driving metal sheets around the perimeter of planting holes will also prevent gopher damage.

Growth stops at harvest and the THC content cannot increase. It will stay the same or decrease after harvest. Proper handling is the key to retaining THC potency. Prolonged periods of light, temperatures above 80°F (27°C), friction from fondling hands, and damp, humid conditions should be avoided because they all degrade the THC. The THC chemical is produced in leaves, flowers, and stalked glandular trichomes, lovingly referred to as "resin glands" or simply "trichomes." Stems and roots may smell like they should be smoked, but contain few mind-bending cannabinoids, if any, and the resin is not very psychoactive.Male plants contain much less THC and are harvested before they pollinate females. Female plants are harvested when trichomes show peak ripeness.Leaves are harvested first. Growers hang plants upside down because it is simple, convenient, and effective– not to drain existing THC-potent resin into the buds. Also, boiling roots to extract THC is crazy!

Leaves

Once the large leaves are fully formed, THC potency has generally peaked out. Smaller leaves around buds continue to develop resin until buds are ripe. Peak potency is retained, as long as leaves are healthy and green; nothing is lost by leaving them on the plant. Harvest leaves if they show signs of disease or rapid yellowing that fertilizer has failed to cure. Once they start to yellow and die, potency decreases somewhat. This is true especially with fan leaves that grow before the buds. The large leaves turn yellow when nitrogen-rich fertilizer is withheld during flowering. Cut the entire leaf, including the leaf stem (petiole) and toss it into a bag. Paper bags breathe well and can be closed by folding over the top. Plastic bags do not breathe, so the top must be left open. If the petiole is left on the stem, it shrivels and dies back. This little bit of dead plant attracts moisture and mold. Removing it will avoid mold problems.Keep the paper bag in a closet or area with 40-60 percent humidity and 60-70°F (15-21°C) temperature. Reach into the bag once or twice a day and stir leaves by hand. Leaves should be dry to the touch in five to seven days.Once dry, place in the freezer to get ready to make Ice-0-Lator hash.

After harvest, marijuana must dry before smoking. Drying converts THC from its non-psychoactive, crude, acidic form to its psychoactive neutral form. In other words, fresh green marijuana will not be very potent. Drying also converts 75 percent or more of the freshly harvested plant into water vapor and other gases. When you cut a plant or plant part and hang it to dry, the transport of fluids within the plant continues, but at a slower rate. Stomata close soon after harvest, and drying is slowed since little water vapor escapes. The natural plant processes slowly come to an end as the plant dries.The outer cells are the first to dry, but fluid still moves from internal cells to supply moisture to outer cells which are dry. When this process occurs properly, plants dry evenly throughout. Removing leaves and large stems upon harvest speeds drying; however, moisture content within the "dried" buds, leaves, and stems is uneven. If buds are dried too quickly, chlorophyll and other pigments, starch, and nitrates are trapped within plant tissue, making it taste "green," burn unevenly, and taste bad. When dried relatively slowly, over five to seven days or longer, moisture evaporates evenly into the air, yielding uniformly dry buds with minimal THC decomposition.Slowly dried buds taste sweet and smoke smooth. Taste and aroma improve when pigments break down. Slow even drying–where moisture content is the same throughout stems, foliage and buds– allows enough time for the pigments to degrade.Hanging entire plants to dry allows this process to take place over time.

Packaging And Storage

Storing cannabis in an airtight environment will preserve aroma, taste, and potency.Use a vacuum sealer to evacuate air in glass jars. Inexpensive vacuum sealers are available in the canning section of grocery and variety stores. Growers report that containers sealed with inexpensive vacuum sealers lose the vacuum after a few days.When properly vacuum-packed, buds will stay as fresh as the day they were sealed in the airtight jar.Vacuum seal the jar, and place it in the refrigerator for storage.Leave it in the refrigerator or a cool, dark, dry place for a month or longer. The taste and potency will be tops! Refrigeration slows decomposition, but, remember, refrigerators have a high humidity level, so the container must be sealed airtight.I just checked the relative humidity and temperature in my refrigerator–65 percent relative humidity and 40°F (5°C). Do not place it in the freezer. Freezing draws moisture to the surface of buds, which can harm resin glands on the surface. Place sealed containers in a cool, dry, dark place. Some growers prefer to keep airtight, sealed containers in the refrigerator. If the seal is not airtight, the low temperature in the refrigerator creates a condition of high humidity. Dry buds stored in a container that is not airtight attract moisture in the high humidity environment. Before long, the buds are so moist that they must be dried again.